Dear Penne,

We hope the [...] you will discover in [...] for yourself what an amazing place China is!

Merry Christmas.

Love,

Adrienne & Dave

2005

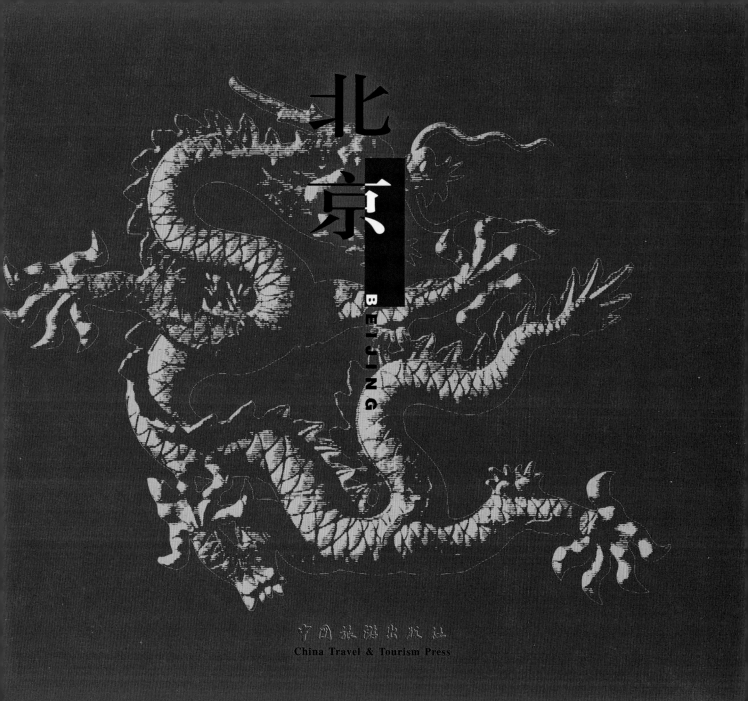

北京

BEIJING

中国旅游出版社

China Travel & Tourism Press

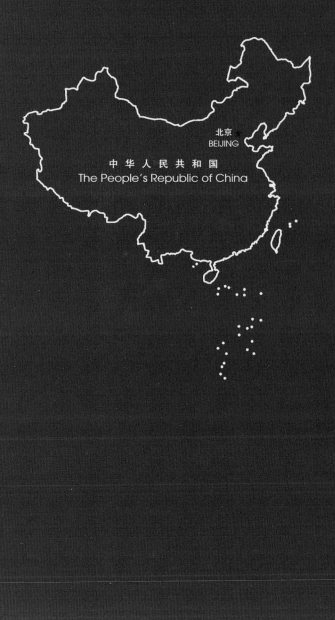

北京
BEIJING

中 华 人 民 共 和 国
The People's Republic of China

责任编辑：秦凤京
撰　　文：王　洋
翻　　译：李建国　鲁安琪
摄　　影：王慧明　王文波　王　耕　王希宝
　　　　　朱　苈　李　佐　刘雅平　陆　岩
　　　　　肖　田　宋　红　严向群　陈　宇
　　　　　姚天新　赵德春　翟东风　胡敦志
　　　　　龚威健　蒙　紫　秦凤京
绘　　图：姚占标
设　　计：多伶平面设计工作室

图书在版编目（CIP）数据

北京／中国旅游出版社编.—北京：中国旅游出版社，
2003.1
　ISBN 7-5032-2095-3

　Ⅰ.北… Ⅱ.中… Ⅲ.名胜古迹—北京市—画册
Ⅳ.K928.701-64

中国版本图书馆 CIP 数据核字（2002）第 087586 号

北京

出版发行：中国旅游出版社
地　　址：北京建国门内大街甲9号
邮政编码：100005
印　　刷：利丰雅高（深圳）印刷有限公司
版　　次：2003年1月第1版
印　　次：2003年1月第1次印刷
开　　本：850×1168 毫米　1/24
印　　张：4
印　　数：5080
005800

TABLE OF CONTENTS

Foreword

这是一座古老却又洋溢着青春活力的城市。这是一座在不同文化的碰撞下焕发出夺目光彩的城市。

北京，中华人民共和国的首都，中国的政治中心和文化中心。

她是世界知名的古城，在人类文明史册中占有重要位置。

北京是一座非凡的城市，她迷人而又有独特的个性。无论是徜徉在有数百年历史的皇宫林苑，还是漫步在灰墙黛瓦的古老街巷，或者伫立在高楼林立的现代化街区，都会有一种惊奇、一份感叹油然涌上您的心头：深厚的文化底蕴和强烈的现代气息怎么会如此融洽地在这个古老而又年轻的城市并存着？！

这就是北京的魅力。

北京很古老。50万年前，北京出现了会用火、有语言、能够直立行走的北京猿人。他们是世界上最早懂得使用火的原始人类之一。

作为一个历史悠久的城市，北京与世界上任何古城相比都毫不逊色。她建城已有3000余年，作为都城也已有800年的历史。自元朝的第二个皇帝忽必烈定都北京开始（1272年），北京第一次成为中国的政治、经济和文化中心。经过二十余年的建设，一座以一连串的湖泊衬托着美丽的宫殿和园林，有着规整的棋盘式街道布局的城市诞生了。她就是元大都，是意大利著名旅行家马可·波罗笔下当时世界上最宏伟壮丽的城市。自那以后，她一直是中国最重要的城市和封建王朝的都城。

北京很美丽。从3000年前一个诸侯国的都邑，到一个有着十几亿人的泱泱大国的首都，数千年各种不同民族文化的融合、数百年帝王之都的熏陶以及近百年东西方文化的碰撞，孕育出成熟大气、凝重醇厚的北京文化。作为中国主流文化中最重要的部分，这种由千年文化积淀陶冶出的、极具地域特色的文化与新世纪的气息交融，形成了奇异而微妙的文化存在，使古城北京体现出一种独特的文化之美。正是这种文化之美，使北京具有了永远的魅力。

数百年来，几代王朝的不断建设，为北京留下了无法计数的名胜古迹和文化艺术珍品，使北京成为拥有世界遗产最多的中国城市。人类建筑史上的奇迹万里长城、世界上现存规模最大的皇家建筑群故宫、如诗如画的皇家园林颐和园和北海、世界上最大的祭祀性建筑群天坛、规模宏大的皇

家墓寝明十三陵、远古北京人的居所周口店猿人洞、埋藏着千年石刻佛经的房山云居寺等等，还有香山、潭柘寺、戒台寺等众多设计精妙的公园和寺庙，北京的名胜古迹多得不胜枚举。而那些呈棋盘状构成北京城基本骨架的上千条胡同，以及有着独特韵味的京味文化，更使北京因融合了古城神韵、皇都气度和多层面的市井文化而具有独树一帜的美丽。

北京又很现代。作为中华人民共和国的首都和中国的政治中心和文化中心，北京城市规模不断扩大，人口不断增加，经济实力不断增强。特别是20世纪80年代以来，北京以海纳百川的胸怀吸引着国内外、海内外的各类人才和投资。北京是全中国吸引外资最多、人才最集中、信息最发达、现代化程度最高的城市。而2008年即将在北京举办的奥运会，更使北京的城市建设和文化建设日新月异，向着国际化的现代都市大步迈进。

到过北京的人，无不惊叹她的独特和大气；而长住在北京的人，却会陶醉在她的深邃和丰富之中。

Foreword

Beijing, capital of People's Republic of China, is the hub of the national political and cultural life.

It is an old city full of vigor. It is also where different cultures meet and melt into one.

It is a well-known tourist destination in the world, taking an important position in the history of human civilization.

Beijing is a unique and charming city with its own features. Wherever you go, either walking in hundred years old imperial palaces and gardens, or strolling on the ancient roads and lanes made of gray wall and black tiles, or ever standing among modern high-rises and skyscrapers, you will find yourself keeping asking how a deep cultural tradition and strong modern breath could harmoniously co-exist in such an old and youthful city.

It is where the charm of Beijing lies.

The history of Beijing can be dated back to 500,000 years ago when Peking man just appeared. Peking man had language and was able to walk, and was one of the earliest human beings who knew how to make use of the fire.

As a city, Beijing has 3,000 years' history, of which more than 800 years serving as a capital. The city became a political, economic and cultural center in China for the first time in history in 1272 when Kublai, the second emperor of the Yuan Dynasty, chose Beijing as capital. A beautiful city with regularly crisscrossed streets and dotted with rivers, lakes, palaces and gardens was gradually born in the following two decades. It was then called Dadu (Grand Capital) in the Yuan Dynasty (1368-1644?), and was described by Marco Polo as the most prosperous and glorious city in the world at that time. It has remained as an important city and capital in China since then.

Beijing is a beautiful city. During the process of its growth from a small town under a seigneur 3,000 years ago to a capital city for a large country with a population of 11 billion, a great and deep culture has been nurtured, and has later become the most important part of the mainstream culture in China. In Beijing culture you may feel the blend of different nationalities, the influence of feudal dynasties and harmonious notes in the cultural conflicts between the East and the West. It is a unique culture featuring thousand years old history, strong local characteristics and fresh breath of the new century. Because of this, the city boasts an everlasting charm.

The continuous construction of the feudal dynasties in several hundred years has left the city numerous places of historical interest and cultural treasures. Beijing is the city which has the most sights listed on the World Heritage List in China. There are many world renown attractions, the Great Wall, a wonder of man-made structure; the Palace Museum, the largest royal building group exist today; the Summer Palace and Beihai Park, the poetic royal gardens; the Temple of Heaven, the largest sacrificial architectural group in the world; the Ming Tombs, the large-size royal burial ground; Ape Man Cave in Zhoukoudian, where Peking man once lived and; Yunju Temple at Fangshan, where thousand-year-old stone carvings of Buddhist sutra can be found. Of course, Beijing has more to show, the Fragrant Hills, Tanzhe Monastery and Jietai Monastery, to name only a few. The crisscrossed streets and lanes that form the basic framework of the ancient city, its left-behind imperial mien and multi-dimensional cultures have put together to make it a city with magic attraction.

Beijing is also a modern city. As a national capital of the People's Republic of China, Beijing's city scale is expanding and at the same time its population and economic strength are also keeping increased. Since the 80's in the 20th century, Beijing has opened its arms to welcome different talents and investments from home and abroad. Beijing is the city that has attracted most of the foreign investments to the country. It now has built a well-developed information network, gathered many talents and has become the most modern city in China. The 2008 Olympic Games is sure to promote the urban and cultural construction of the city and accelerate its process toward an international metropolis.

No one will pass Beijing without exclaiming its uniqueness and greatness. Beijing residents also feel honored to live in a city with rich and deep cultural connotations.

北京的心脏
Heart of Beijing

　　对中国人来说，也许没有一个地方像天安门广场那样令人魂牵梦萦。她是百余年来中华民族许多重大历史事件的见证，她是自信、自立的中华人民共和国的象征，她是北京的心脏。

　　Probably, there is not any place as ravishing (enchanting) as Tian'anmen Square in China. The square has witnessed many historic events for centuries. It is the heart of Beijing and also a symbol of confidence and self-reliance of the People's Republic of China.

天安门城楼
Tian'anmen Rostrum

　　坐落在天安门广场北端的天安门城楼始建于明永乐十五年（1417年），是昔日的皇宫——紫禁城的正门。明、清两朝，它最大的用途是国家有重大庆典，如皇帝登极、册立皇后时在此举行"颁诏"仪式。1949年10月1日，毛泽东主席在天安门城楼上庄严宣布中华人民共和国成立。

　　Built in the Ming Dynasty in 1417, Tian'anmen Rostrum, which is located in the north of the square, was formally the entrance to the Forbidden City where emperors of the Ming and Qing dynasties held grand ceremonies. It was on this rostrum late Chairman Mao Zedong announced to the world the founding of the People's Republic of China on October 1, 1949.

　　中华人民共和国的国旗——五星红旗在天安门广场上空高高飘扬。每天黎明和黄昏，许多人会肃立在五星红旗周围，等待庄严的升、降国旗仪式。

　　The Five-Starred Red Flag, the national flag of the People's Republic of China, is flying high over the square. The daily flag raising and lowering ceremonies at sunrise and sunset always attract many people.

天安门广场南北长880米，东西宽500米，总面积达44万平方米，可容纳100万人举行盛大集会，是世界最大的广场。天安门广场的东侧是中国历史博物馆和中国革命博物馆，西侧是人民大会堂；广场中央高高矗立的人民英雄纪念碑记录着百余年来中国人民民族解放的艰苦历程。纪念碑南侧的毛主席纪念堂于1977年落成。每天，有成千上万来自全国和世界各地的人们到天安门广场参观、游览。

Tian'anmen Square is the largest of the sort in the world. It is 880 meters long from north to south, and 500 meters wide from east to west. Occupying an area of 440,000 square meters, it can accommodate a large size assembly for one million people. To the east is the Chinese History Museum and Chinese Revolutionary Museum. To the west is the Great Hall of People. In the middle of square is the Monument to the People's Heroes, which has recorded Chinese people's hard struggles for the national liberation. Back to the south is the Chairman Mao Memorial Hall built in 1977. Each day many tourists from home and abroad will come to pay homage to him.

人民大会堂
The Great Hall of People

人民大会堂建成于1959年,总面积172万平方米,是全国人民代表大会常务委员会的办公地点。这座由中央大厅、万人大会堂、7000平方米的大宴会厅,以及以包括港澳台在内的全国各省、自治区、直辖市的名称命名的厅堂组成的宏大建筑群,当年建设只用了令人难以置信的10个月的时间。

The Great Hall of People, built in 1959, occupying an area of 1.72 million square meters, is the seat for the Standing Committee of the National People's Congress. It is a great architectural group consisting of Central Hall, Ten-Thousand-People Conference Hall, 7,000-square-meter banquet hall and halls named after provinces, autonomous regions and cities directly under the jurisdiction of the Central Government. The construction of the building only took 10 months.

中国革命博物馆、中国历史博物馆
The Chinese Revolutionary Museum & The Chinese History Museum

中国革命博物馆是中国目前革命文物收藏量最大的博物馆,展出的4500多件实物、文献、图片、绘画、模型、雕塑生动地再现了自1840年起的中国近、现代史进程。

中国历史博物馆展厅面积约9000多平方米,馆内有文物藏品30余万件,展示了中国自原始社会起至封建社会(1840年前)5000年的文明史。

The Chinese Revolutionary Museum has the largest collection of the revolutionary relics in the country. 4,500 items on show have vividly represented a modern and contemporary China since 1840.

The Chinese History Museum has 9,000 square meters displaying ground. It houses more than 300,000 cultural relics that have well displayed China's 5,000 years of civilization from the Primary Society to the Feudal Society (before 1840).

毛主席纪念堂
Chairman Mao Zedong Memorial Hall

　　毛主席纪念堂于1979年开放，每天都有许许多多的人满怀崇敬之心前往瞻仰一代伟人的遗容。

　　Chairman Mao Zedong Memorial Hall was open in 1979. Everyday, many people will come to pay homage to this great man.

人民英雄纪念碑
The Monument to the People's Heroes

　　1958年，为纪念自1840年至1949年百余年间为了中华民族的解放而牺牲的先烈，在天安门广场的中央，建造起碑高37.94米，碑基3000余平方米的人民英雄纪念碑。碑的正面是毛主席题写的"人民英雄永垂不朽"8个镏金大字，背面是周恩来总理题写的碑文。碑座上的8幅大型汉白玉浮雕概括了中国百余年来重要的历史事件。

　　The Monument to the People's Heroes was set up in 1958 to commemorate martyrs sacrificed for the course of national liberation during the period of 1840 to 1949. There are late Chairman Mao's golden inscriptions of "the heroes of the people are immortal"on the front side. The article on the backside was written by late Premier Zhou Enlai. The eight large marble carvings in relief outline the important historic events happened in Chinese history in more than one hundred years.

天安门广场鸟瞰
A bird's eye view of Tian'anmen Square

节日的天安门广场花团锦簇
Tian'anmen Square becomes a sea of flowers on festivals.

皇家宫苑
Imperial Palaces and Gardens

　　金碧辉煌的皇家宫殿群，优美典雅的皇家园林以及延续数千年而不断的文化底蕴是北京的骄傲。从世界各地来到北京的旅游者无不希望亲眼目睹那些世界闻名的历史遗存。

　　Golden and bright imperial palaces, graceful imperial gardens and a thousand-year-old culture and world-renowned historical monuments are the pride of Beijing and are what tourists are eager to see and explore.

故宫

Palace Museum

　　故宫曾被称作紫禁城，是明、清两朝（1403年－1911年）的皇宫，始建于明永乐四年（1406年），历15年建成。故宫东西宽750米，南北长960米，总面积为72万平方米，有房屋近万间，是世界上现存规模最大、保存最完好的皇宫，其建筑风格集中体现了中国建筑的传统和特点，是中国古代建筑的杰作。故宫内藏有明清两个朝代的上千万件档案、书籍和上百万件珍宝、艺术品，其中有许多孤品，是中国最大的博物馆和珍宝馆。1925年，故宫改为博物院，对公众开放；1987年，被列入《世界遗产》名录。

The Imperial Palace, also known as the Forbidden City, was the imperial palace of the Ming and Qing dynasties. It is 960 meters long from north to south and 750 meters wide from east to south. It is the largest and best-preserved imperial palace existing in the world, with approximately 10,000 rooms in the 720,000-square-meter compound. It is a masterpiece of traditional Chinese architectural works. The Imperial Palace houses some 10,000 books and archives of the Ming and Qing dynasties, many are the only existing copies, and some 1,000,000 pieces of treasures and artworks, and is therefore the largest museum and treasure house in China. It changed its name as the Palace Museum and opened to the public in 1925. It was listed as a world cultural heritage in 1987.

太和殿晴雪
Hall of Supreme Harmony on a fine day after snow

　　故宫基本上可以分为两大部分，即：外朝和内廷。外朝主体建筑有"三大殿"：太和殿、中和殿、保和殿以及侧殿：文华殿和武英殿。"三大殿"是皇帝举行盛大典礼、行使权力及与群臣共议国是的主要场所。

The Palace Museum is basically divided into two parts of the palace court and the inner court. In the palace court there are the Hall of Supreme Harmony, the Hall of Complete Harmony, the Hall of Preserving Harmony and two wing halls of Wenhua and Wuying. The three main halls were where emperors held grand ceremonies, exerted rights and discussed national affairs with the ministers.

中和殿（前）与保和殿（后）
Hall of Complete Harmony (front) and Hall of Preserving Harmony (back)

太和殿俗称金銮殿，是明清皇帝举行重要典礼的大殿，在"三大殿"中规模最大，规格最高。

大殿中设雕龙镂空金漆宝座，殿内梁、枋全部沥粉贴金。靠近宝座的六根沥粉蟠龙金柱与宝座上方的金漆蟠龙吊珠藻井，更是充分显示出皇帝的赫赫威仪。

Hall of Supreme Harmony, also known as Jinluan Hall, was the place where emperors of the Ming and Qing dynasties held grand ceremonies. It is the largest in size and scale among the three great halls in the Palace Museum. The throne carved with dragons and decorated with gold is in the middle of the hall. Gilded beams, the six gilded coiling-dragon pillars near the throne and the gilded coiling-dragon caisson ceiling over the throne conspire the majesty of the imperial power.

内廷包括乾清宫、交泰殿、坤宁宫、御花园以及东六宫和西六宫。这里是皇帝处理日常政务以及和嫔妃们居住的地方。乾清宫内的"正大光明"匾是清代自雍正皇帝确立秘密建储制度后，皇帝存放建储密诏的地方。

The Palace of Heavenly Purity, Hall of Union and Peace, Palace of Earthly Tranquility, Imperial Garden, six east palaces and six west palaces are located in the inner court, where the emperors managed the daily affairs and concubines lived. A plaque bearing an inscription of "be open and aboveboard" was where emperors hid away their secret imperial edicts to ordain the crown prince after a secret accreditation system had been set up.

乾清宫门外威武的金狮
The golden lions at the entrance of the Hall of Heavenly Purity

养心殿位于故宫西路，是雍正以后皇帝的寝宫和处理政务的地方
The Hall of Yangxin, on the west route of the Palace Museum, was where Emperor Yong Zheng Slept and handled national affairs.

坤宁宫东暖阁，皇帝大婚的洞房
Dongnuange at the Palace of Earthly Tranquility was the bridal chamber of emperors.

乾隆皇帝朝服像
Emperor Qian Long

储秀宫是故宫西六宫之一，慈禧太后晚年曾在这里居住
Chuxiu Palace, one of the six west palaces, was where Empress Dowager Cixi once lived in her late years.

养心殿东暖阁，慈禧太后在这里垂帘听政
Empress Dowager Cixi, who had abdicated to Dongnuange at the Palace of Earthly Tranquility, was still the person at the helm of the Qing Empire.

长春宫寝宫，慈禧曾居此宫
Empress Dowager once lived in the Bedchamber in Changchun Palace.

慈禧太后画像
Portrait of Empress Dowager Cixi

北海

Beihai Park

北海是800年前的金朝皇帝按照中国民间"海上仙山"的传说兴建的，历经金、元、明、清几代王朝的建设。北海的面积只有68.2万平方米，但其对于中国园林"移地缩天"原理的运用却是淋漓尽致。这个建筑精巧、布局紧凑、湖光山色的皇家园林有着世界上面积最小的城——团城、五彩斑斓的琉璃影壁——九龙壁、被誉为"海上蓬莱"的琼华岛和美丽的白塔，以及蜿蜒于碧波之上的五龙亭和小巧玲珑、被称为"园中之园"的静心斋等景区，宛若市井之中的一片净土，令人流连忘返。

Beihai Park was built 800 years ago according to the legendary "fairy mountain on the sea". In the 68.2 hectare elegant park, you may see the Round City, the smallest city in the world; the Nine Dragon Screen, made of colorful glazed tiles; Qionghua Isle, reputed as a fairy land on the sea; beautiful White Pagoda; Five Dragon Pagodas on the lake and Jingxinzhai, a garden within the garden. It is a popular park among Beijingers and tourists alike. Viewing Qionghua Islet from a distance.

用彩色琉璃制成的九龙壁气势非凡，九条龙鲜明灵动，似要破壁而出，堪称华夏琉璃的经典之作。

The dragons on the Nine Dragon Screen are vividly portrayed that it seems that they are about to fly out of the screen at any moment.

静心斋是北海的"园中之园"，以小中见大、玲珑幽静为特色。

Jinxinzhai featuring tranquility and exquisiteness is the garden within the garden.

团城承光殿内供奉的玉佛高1.5米，系用一整块玉雕刻而成，雍容华贵、精美绝伦，是清光绪皇帝年间缅甸进贡的。

The jade Buddha enshrined in the Chengguang Hall in the Round city is 1.5 meters high. It is carved out from a single piece of jade. It is said that the exquisite sculpture was paid as a tribute from Burma during the reign of Emperor Guangxu in the Qing Dynasty.

景山

Jingshan Park

　　位于故宫北部，因此被称作"故宫的后花园"。景山始建于元代，明初叫万岁山，清顺治十二年（1655年）改名景山。东侧山下原有一棵古槐树，明朝最后一位皇帝——崇祯皇帝在李自成农民军攻进紫禁城时，走投无路在古槐树上吊自尽。古槐树已死，现在的槐树是后人补栽的。现在，景山是北京内城全景的最佳观赏处，傍晚时分在景山最高处的万春亭俯瞰北京，近处，紫禁城金碧辉煌、气势恢弘；远方，高楼大厦鳞次栉比，气象万千。

　　Located to the north of the Palace Museum, it is called the rear garden of the Palace Museum. The park was first built in the Yuan Dynasty. It was called Longevity Hill in the early years of the Ming Dynasty. It got its present name in 1655. At eastern foot of the hill, there was an aged Chinese scholar tree. Emperor Chongzheng of the Ming Dynasty hanged himself by the tree when the army of peasant uprising occupied the Forbidden City. The original tree died and a new tree has been planted in its place. Now, Jingshan is the best place to view the city. Standing in the Wanchun Pavilion on the Jingshan Hill when the sun gets set, you can view a grand Forbidden City bathing in golden sunlights and forests of high-rises in the city.

景山牡丹园
The Peony Garden at Jingshan Park

天坛

The Temple of Heaven

天坛是世界上最大的皇家祭天建筑，始建于明代永乐十八年（1420年），面积273万平方米，是世界上最独特的建筑群之一。她不仅完整地表达了中国人对天、地、神的崇拜，而且反映了古代中国人朴素的宇宙观和高超的建筑艺术。1998年12月，天坛被列入《世界遗产》名录。

天坛由两道"回"字形的坛墙分为外坛和内坛，根据中国人"天圆地方"的传统观念，北面的坛墙呈半圆形，象征"天"；南面的坛墙为方形，象征"地"。天坛的主要建筑分布在内坛，北边以祈年殿为中心的一组建筑群叫祈谷坛，皇帝在这里举行祈谷大典，祈求丰年；南面以圜丘、皇穹宇为主的一组建筑群叫圜丘坛，每年冬季，皇帝在这里举行祭天大典。在内坛西侧，还有一组建筑群叫作斋宫，举行祭天仪式前，皇帝先要在斋宫戒斋、沐浴，以示虔诚。

明清两朝，作为皇家的祭天场所，天坛广植松柏。今天，随处可见的百年松柏与庄严神秘的祭坛一起营造出一种古朴典雅、祥和宁静的氛围，使天坛更具魅力。

Built in 1420, occupying an area of 273 hectares, the Temple of Heaven is the largest imperial architecture for worshiping heaven in the world, and one of the most unique architectural groups in the world as well. It not only completely expresses the adoration of Chinese people towards the heaven, the earth and the divinities, but also reflects the simple concept of the universe of Chinese people in ancient times and the high artistic level Chinese people had achieved in architecture several hundred years ago. The Temple of Heaven was listed on the World Heritage List by the UNESCO in December 1998.

The Temple of Heaven is divided into two parts of the outer altar and inner alter by two "U" walls. According to traditional Chinese concept of "circular heaven and square earth", the wall in the north is circular, symbolizing the heaven, while the wall in the south is square, implying the earth. The major buildings are located in the inner alter. To the north of the complex is the Hall of Prayer for Good Harvest, a magnificent piece mounted on a three-tiered marble terrace, was where emperors held grand ceremonies to pray for good harvests. To the south of the complex are the Round Altar and the Imperial Vault of Heaven, where emperors held sacrificial rites. To the west complex is the Hall of Abstinence, where the emperors would prepare themselves for the solemn occasion by spending a night fasting.

As an imperial sacrificial ground in the Ming and Qing dynasties, pines and cypress were densely planted. Today, tourists can still feel the solemn and quite atmosphere created by the mystic altars and old trees.

祈年殿是一座无与伦比的建
筑。这座高38米、直径32.72米的
圆形建筑仅凭木榫交接，斗拱支
架，不用一根铁钉，就完成了奇妙
的架构，是中国木结构建筑的登峰
造极之作。殿内的4根楠木大柱象
征四季，12根朱漆金柱代表了12个
月，体现了中国古代对于天文历法
的精确计算与研究水平。

The Hall of Prayer for Good
Harvest is a unique structure. It is not
only splendid in outer appearance,
but also unique in inner frame. The
entire structure is supported by 28
massive wooden pillars and a
number of bars, laths, joints and
rafters. Not a single iron nail was
used. The four central nanmao pillars
represent the four seasons. There are
two rings of pillars each has twelve
pillars, the inner ring symbolizing the
twelve months and the outer ring the
twelve divisions of the day and night.

皇穹宇是存放神位的地方。这座被蓝琉璃瓦覆盖的圆形建筑高 19.5 米，直径 15.6 米。皇穹宇最奇妙的部分是回音壁：站在皇穹宇围墙边小声说话，相隔十余米，站在围墙另一边的人能够清晰地听到。这说明，500 年前的中国人已经能够将声学原理运用于建筑之中。

The Imperial Vault of Heaven was used to contain tablets of the emperor's ancestors. It is a circular building, 19.5 meters high and 15.6 meters in diameters, covered with blue glazed tiles. The most wonderful part is the Echo Wall, which enables a whisper to travel clearly from one end to the other. This indicates that Chinese people had already known how to apply the acoustic theory into buildings as early as 500 years ago.

圈丘坛棂星门
Lingxing Gate at the Circular Mound Altar

斋宫的正殿——无梁殿
The Beamless Hall, the main hall in the Hall of Abstinence

　　圈丘坛高5米，直径23米。坛中央是一块圆石，被9圈扇形石板围绕，从最中间的9块开始，按9的倍数向外扩展，第9圈为81块。当年，皇帝就站在中央的那块圆石上祭天。

　　Circular Mound Altar is five meters high and 23 meters in diameters. At the center of the altar lies a round stone surrounded by nine concentric rings of stones. The number of stones in the innermost ring is nine, in the second ring 18 and so on, up to the 81 in the ninth ring. Emperors stood in that round stone in the center to worship.

颐和园

Summer Palace

　　颐和园是清朝皇家园林，总面积达290万平方米。颐和园始建于清乾隆年间，原名清漪园。1860年被英法联军焚毁。光绪十四年（1888年），慈禧太后挪用海军经费重修，并改名为颐和园。1998年颐和园被联合国教科文组织列入《世界遗产》名录。

　　颐和园又被称为"夏宫"，是清朝皇帝夏季避暑和处理政务的地方。她巧借自然山水修建，主体景观以宏伟的万寿山佛香阁为中心递次铺开，依山就势，错落有致，美丽壮观。面积达220万平方米的昆明湖为这座世界名园凭添了灵秀之气。从湖上眺望万寿山、佛香阁，湖光山色犹如一幅立体画卷，令人陶醉。颐和园浓缩了北方园林的壮美和南方园林的绮丽，既有人工妙算，却又浑然天成，集中了中国园林建筑的精华，堪称中国园林的博物馆。

　　The original Summer Palace was laid out in 1750, and was burn down by British and French allied forces during the second Opium War (1860). Empress Dowager Cixi had it rebuilt in 1888 with funds for navy development. It was then renamed as the Summer Palace.The Summer Palacewas listed on the World Heritage List by the UNESCO in December 1998.

　　The Summer Palace served as summer residences of the imperial households. The Summer Palace is huge, some 2.5 km from east to west, most of it being taken up by Kunming Lake. Longevity Hill is the focal point of the Summer Palace. The panoramic view from the summit is well worth the climb. On top of the Longevity Hill are several Buddhist temples. The Summer Palace is a blend of north gardens and south gardens. It is actually a museum of Chinese gardens with collections of masterpieces of garden building in China.

颐和园秋韵
Autumn in the Summer Palace

佛香阁是一座三层八面四重檐的木结构建筑，高41米，是观览颐和园全景的最佳处。

Tower of Buddhist Incense is a three-tier. four-layer-eave octagonal wooden structure. The 41 meters high tower proves to be a best spot to see a panoramic view of the Summer Palace.

石坊又名清晏舫，石砌船身，上为木结构西式楼舱

The main body of the Marble Boat is built of marble. The superstructure is made of wood and built in the western architectural style.

乐寿堂，慈禧太后在颐和园的寝宫
Hall of Happiness and Longevity, Empress Dowager Cixi's bedroom in the Summer Palace.

　　万寿山的后山，温雅秀丽、酷似江南水乡的苏州街和按照佛教意境建造的四大部洲，与山前的宏大华丽形成了鲜明对照。
　　At the backside of the Longevity Hill, there are Suzhou Street, a model of water town in south China, and Four Great Continents built in Buddhist conception.

玉澜堂，光绪皇帝在颐和园的寝宫
Hall of Jade Ripples, Emperor Guanxu's bedroom in the Summer Palace.

　　拥有 273 间、长达 728 米、绘有 14000 幅苏式彩画的长廊，像一条彩练串联起万寿山和东宫门的宫殿区。
　　The Long Corridor is 728 meters long with 273 sections. The beams of the corridor are painted with more than 14,000 paintings. It likes a silk ribbon connecting the Longevity Hill with the palaces at the East Palace Gate.

名胜古迹
Places of Historical Interest

无论是旅游者还是长住北京的居民,北京的名胜古迹对他们都具有长久的吸引力。历尽沧桑的古迹成为今天的名胜,像一部浓缩的历史,引人去阅读、去品味。

Places of historical interest have strong attraction toward Beijing residents and tourists alike. These historical monuments just like a condensed history book inviting you to read and explore.

长城
Great Wall

中国有一句堪称家喻户晓的民间俗语"不到长城非好汉",这句话现在也成了来中国旅游的外国旅游者人人皆知的名言。被誉为世界建筑史奇迹的万里长城在北京北部山区绵延600余公里,像一座屏障,保护着古代中国的首都不会受到异族的侵扰。这个始建于2000余年前的人类最伟大的工程在北京留下了其最壮观、最精华的部分。作为拱卫京师的军事要冲,北京地区的八达岭、慕田峪、司马台长城在明成祖年间重修,现在是北京最有吸引力的旅游名胜。1987年,万里长城被列入了《世界遗产》名录。

"You are not a great man yet before you climb the Great Wall". In China, nearly every tourist knows the famous Chinese saying. The wall, zigzagging for about 600 kilometers in the mountainous area in the north part of Beijing, protected the ancient capital from invasions. The greatest man-made structure on earth has its most wonderful sections in Beijing. As strategic important posts, the Badaling, Mutianyu and Simatai sections were reconstructed during the Ming Dynasty. Now they have become highlights of a Beijing tour. The Great Wall was put on the World Heritage List by the UNESCO in 1987.

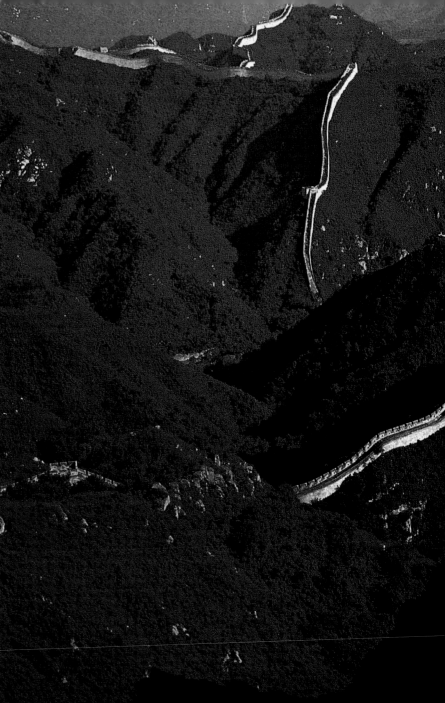

八达岭长城是长城最著名的地段，位于北京西北延庆县关沟北口，是扼守京北的咽喉要道。长城起伏蜿蜒，如苍龙凌空飞舞，雄伟壮观。

Badaling is the most well-known section of the Great Wall. Located in Yanqing County, northwest of Beijing, it is a strategically important place in the north of Beijing. The winding wall here resembles a dragon preparing to take off at any moment.

长城与山石形成一体，十分坚固。
The wall and the stones have become a solid entity.

　　如果说八达岭长城的特色是雄伟，那么，慕田峪长城的特色就是秀丽。慕田峪位于北京东北郊的怀柔区，这一带植被繁茂，春花秋叶、夏荫冬雪，长城四季景色不同，极具观赏价值。

If you use the word "spectacular" to describe the Badaling, then the word you chose for the Mutianyu will probably be "elegant". Mutianyu is located in Huairou District in northeast of the city, where it is densely covered with rich vegetation. The scenery at Mutianyu Section changes with seasons.

　　慕田峪长城的建筑很独特，城墙多为双面垛口，敌楼密集，便于防御。特别是箭扣一带，长城往往矗立在绝壁之上，给人〝无限风光在险峰〞之感。

The construction of the Mutianyu Section of the wall is very unique. Most section of the wall has a double battlement. Towers are densely built for defensive purpose. The section near Jiankou is almost built on the cliff.

山舞〝银龙〞
A Silver Dragon.

雾锁箭扣
Jiankou in fog

历尽沧桑
Witnessing changes
of history.

司马台长城蜿蜒于北京东北郊区密云县境内的崇山峻岭之上，以险峻著称。这一带峰峦起伏连绵，长城依山势建在山脊之上，城墙及敌楼的形式变化多端，被专家认为是＂中国长城之最＂。

The Shimatai Section of the wall winds along the rising and falling steep mountains in Miyun County in the northeast suburb of Beijing. Different types of parapets and towers show at this section of the wall, hence it is regarded by experts as the section of the wall with most variations.

司马台长城最高海拔为986米，绝壁之上，一座敌楼兀立峰巅。民间传说晴天的夜晚，站在敌楼上可以望见京城的灯火，因而得名望京楼。

The highest point of the Shimatai Section is at Wangjin (Viewing Beijing) Tower built on a cliff 986 meters above sea level. It is said that standing on the tower on a fine day night, you can view lights from Beijing.

居庸关是万里长城中最著名的关隘之一，在北京城西北50公里处，地势绝险，景色迷人。

Located 50 kilometers northwest of Beijing, Jurongguan Section of the wall featuring rugged topography and beautiful scenery is the most well-known section of the Great Wall.

云台
Cloud Terrace

　　居庸关保存有元代遗留下来的汉白玉云台，上面精美的元代浮雕和用六种文字撰写的陀罗尼经的经文具有很高的文物价值和艺术欣赏价值。

　　It has well-preserved Marble Cloudy Platform of the Yuan Dynasty. Exquisite carvings in relief and Tuluonijin lection written in six languages can be found on the platform. It has a high value both as cultural relics and work of art.

十三陵
Ming Tombs

　　从北京城向北行50公里，天寿山脚下有一片排列成弧状的金碧辉煌的建筑群，这就是明代皇帝的陵寝十三陵。十三陵埋葬着明朝的13位皇帝、23位皇后，距今已有500余年的历史。每座陵墓由棱恩殿、明楼（又称宝顶）和地宫（陵墓）组成。十三陵中最大的陵是长陵，它是明朝第三个皇帝明成祖朱棣的陵寝，其棱恩殿的规模与故宫的太和殿相仿。现在，明十三陵中只有定陵已被挖掘、开放，游客可以进入地宫，一睹明代皇帝的丧葬方式和被发掘出来的精美文物。

　　50 kilometers north of Beijing, at the foot of the Tianshuo Mountain, there is a resplendent and magnificent architectural group. It is the Ming Tombs where 13 Ming emperors and 23 empresses were buried. Each tomb has a Ling'an Hall, a Ming Tower and a underground palace. Changling is the tomb of Zhu Li, the third emperor of the Ming Dynasty. It is the largest among the 13 tombs. Ling'an Hall in Changling is as big as the Hall of Supreme Harmony at the Palace Museum. So far, Only Dingling has been excavated and opened to tourist. Tourists may walk into the underground palace to see excavated cultural relics.

定陵埋葬着明万历皇帝朱翊钧和他的两位皇后。地宫面积达1195平方米，为石拱券无梁结构。地宫中出土的3000余件文物，件件精美绝伦，反映了中国的纺织、雕刻、铸造和编织等工艺在明代已达到了非常高的水平。

Dingling buries Emperor Wanli and two of his empresses. The 1,195-square-meter underground palace is a beamless stone structure. More than 3,000 cultural relics unearthed reflect that technology in textile, carving, casting and weaving in China in the Ming Dynasty has already achieved a very high level.

定陵出土的凤冠
Phoenix coronet unearthed from the Dingling.

整个陵区从一座有五门六柱十一楼的石牌坊开始，一条长达7公里、纵贯陵区的神路将13个陵墓联接起来。神路的石像生——12尊石人、24尊石兽雕工精美，虽经600年风霜雨雪，仍然栩栩如生，令人惊叹。

The whole tomb area starts from a stone archway and is linked by a seven-kilometer-long road flanked by stone statures, 12 generals and 24 animals. Witnessing different weathers in 500 years, they still look very vivid today.

香山
Fragrant Hills

　　香山位于北京城的西部，是一处著名的园林风景区，最高峰海拔557米，因难于攀登被称作"鬼见愁"。香山满山遍植枫树、黄栌，每当秋季来临，层林尽染，万山红遍，游人争相前往观赏。

Located in the west of Beijing, it is a well-known scenic spot. The highest peak is Guijianchou, 557 meters above sea level. Maple trees are widely plants on the hills. In autumn, the frosted leaves will dye the hills into a yellowish red world.

圆明园
Yuanmingyuan

圆明园是环绕福海的圆明、万春、长春三园的总称，位于颐和园东侧，是比颐和园还大的皇家御园，圆明园占地约350万平方米，因面积最大、景点最多、最精美而被称为"万园之园"。1860年被入侵北京的英法联军焚毁，1983年开辟成遗址公园。

Yuanmingyuan, also known as the Garden of Perfection and Brightness, is located to the east of the Summer Palace. It included three hills and five gardens, and was once called "the top garden among ten thousand gardens" for its large scale, wealth of attractions and exquisite workmanship. It was burned down in 1860 by the British and French allied army. It has opened as a ruin park since 1983.

雍和宫

Yonghe Lamasery

　　为了巩固多民族的国家，清朝皇帝十分注重与西藏、蒙古的贵族和宗教界的关系。清朝皇帝曾数次接见藏区宗教领袖，并将北京的一座王府——雍和宫改为喇嘛庙。

　　雍和宫初建于清康熙三十三年（1694年），曾是雍正皇帝继位前的府邸。乾隆九年（1744年），雍和宫正式改为喇嘛庙，成为清政府管理全国喇嘛教事务的中心。

　　雍和宫有藏传佛教博物馆之称，保存有大量的佛教文物和资料、图片。雍和宫万佛阁供奉的木雕弥勒菩萨像由一整根白檀香木雕刻而成，直径3米，高18米，加上埋在地下的8米，共有26米高。传说这根巨大无比的白檀香木来自尼泊尔，七世达赖喇嘛将它运至京城用了三年的时间。

To consolidate the multi-nationality country, the Qing emperors attached much importance to the relationships with Tibetan and Mongolian nobles and important figures in religious world. Emperors in the Qing Dynasty met with religious leaders from Tibet several times, and ordered a prince's mansion changed into a lamasery. Yonghe Lamasery was first built in 1694, on the site of Emperor Yongzheng's mansion before he succeed to the throne. In 1744, the name of Yonghe Lamasery was officially used and the lamasery became a center for the Qing governor to manage Lamaism affairs in the country.

Yonghe Lamasery keeps a lot of Buddhist cultural relics, documents and photos and is called the "museum of Tibetan Buddhism". The Mandala Buddha enshrined in Ten-Thousand-Buddha Tower is 26 meters high and three meters in diameters, and was carved out a single piece of sandal wood transported to Beijing from Nepal by the seventh Dalai Lama in three years time.

每年农历正月二十九至二月初一，雍和宫都要"打鬼"。"打鬼"是喇嘛教的一种宗教仪式，藏语叫做"跳布扎"，即由僧侣装扮成鬼神的模样表演宗教舞蹈。

On every twenty-ninth day in the first lunar month and first day in the second lunar month in Chinese lunar calendar, Yonghe Lamasery will "beat ghosts". It is a religious rite of Lamaism and called "tiaobuzha" in Tibetan. On the occasion, religious dances will be performed by monks made up as ghosts and divinities.

雍和宫山门
Entrance to the Yonghe Lamasery.

潭柘寺
Tanzhe Monastry

潭柘寺是北京地区历史最悠久的寺庙，最早建于晋代（265年～317年），比北京城还要古老。北京古称幽州，因而民间早有"先有潭柘，后有幽州"之说。

Tanzhe Monastry, came into being in the Jin Dynasty (265-317) before the forming of Beijing city, is the oldest temple in Beijing.

戒台寺
Jietai Monastry

戒台寺距潭柘寺不远，始建于唐武德五年（662年），以全国寺庙最大的戒台和古树、奇松著称。

Jietai Monastry is near Tanzhe Monastry. Jietai was built in 662 and is known for its largest Abstinence Platform in the country and its ancient trees and exotic pine trees.

法海寺
Fahai Temple

法海寺在北京城西的石景山区，明正统八年（1443年）建成。寺庙坐落于群山环抱之中，环境清幽秀丽，所存文物众多，并存有三棵古柏。

Fahai Temple, located in Shijingshan District in west of Beijing, was built in the 15th century. The temple is surrounded by mountains and features tranquil environment, rich cultural relics and three ancient cypress trees.

法海寺大雄宝殿内绘有大型壁画，为明代皇家画师绘于正统八年（1443年）。壁画用沥粉贴金，十分华贵精美，是中国明代壁画的最高典范，亦是不可多得的古代艺术珍宝。

The large-scale fresco on the wall of the Precious Hall of the Great Hero at Fahai Temple was painted in 1443. It represents the highest level of fresco art achieved in the Ming Dynasty.

云居寺
The Yunju Temple

云居寺位于北京城西南房山区的白云山麓。公元六世纪的隋代，一位名叫静琬的高僧，为使佛经世代留存而发愿刻经。自静琬和尚起，历代有僧人和石匠到云居寺雕刻石经，前后延续了千余年，留下了隋唐辽金元明各朝所刻石经版14620块，因此，云居寺被称作"北京的敦煌"，房山石经也被称作"石刻长城"。

The Yunju Temple is located at the foot of White Cloud Mountain in Fangshan District in southwest of Beijing. In the Sixth century BC, Jingwan, an accomplished monk vowed to pass the Buddhist scripture generations after generations, began to carve the scripture on stones. In the following one thousand years, monks and craftsmen kept coming to continue the work. Now there are altogether 14,620 pieces of slabstones carved with Buddhist scripture. The temple is called "Dunhuang at Beijing "and the scripture is called " stone carved Great Wall".

孔庙
Confucius Temple

孔庙位于东城区的国子监街，始建于元代，清光绪年间重修扩建，是全国第二大孔庙。

Confucius Temple, situated on the Guozijian Street, is the second largest Confucius temple in China. It was first built in the Yuan Dynasty and was later renovated and expanded in the 19th century.

古观象台
Ancient Observatory

　　北京的古观象台是世界著名观象台之一，建于明正统七年（1442年）。从那时起至1929年，古观象台保持了连续487年的天文观测纪录。那些造型精美、铸造精密的大型铜制天文仪器是中国古代天文学的骄傲。

　　Beijing Ancient Observatory is one of the well-known observatories in the world. It was built in 1442. Since then it had kept continued astronomical observations for 487days until 1929. The fine cast large-size copper equipment is the pride of ancient Chinese astronomy.

北京猿人遗址
The Site of Peking Man

位于北京西南郊的周口店。1929 年 12 月，人类学家在周口店的一个山洞里发现了生活在 50—70 万年，能直立行走、会制造工具、会使用火的北京猿人化石，以及他们的生活痕迹。

The Site of Peking Man is located in the southwest suburb of Beijing. In December 1929 in a small cave near Zhoukoudian anthropologists discovered fossils of Peking Man, who lived about 500,00 to 700,000 years ago, was already able to walk erect and knew how to make tools and fires. Trails of Peking Man's life was also found there.

明城墙
Ming Dynasty City Wall

　　在崇文门与东便门之间，有一段已有500余年历史的明城墙。这是北京明清古城墙中仅存的一部分，2002年，北京市将这里修建成开放式的明城墙遗址公园。

Located between Chongwenmen and Dongbianmen, the remains of the Ming Dynasty City Wall has a history of over 500 years. It is the only section of ancient city wall left behind from the Ming and Qing dynasties in Beijing. A remains park was built along the street in 2002.

菖莆河
The Changpu River

　　菖蒲河也称外金水河，源自皇城西苑中海，流经天安门前，沿皇城南墙内汇入御河，现辟为菖蒲河公园。

The Changpu River, also known as the Outside Golden Water River, starts from the West Garden in the Imperial City, flanks the south wall of the Imperial City and finally converges itself with the Yuhe River. Now a park named after the Changpu River has been built on the site.3

京味文化
Beijing Culture

　　许多到北京旅游的人，都喜欢逛北京的胡同，尝北京的烤鸭和小吃，听北京的京剧，甚至到公园里和自娱自乐的老北京一起唱上几段戏，觉得那才是品味了京味文化。

　　到底什么是京味文化呢？京味文化是指以原来的北京内城为根基，带有明显的北京地区特色的文学、艺术、建筑、语言、民俗以及处世哲学等内容的文化现象，其特点是兼容并蓄、宽厚平和、幽默达观。而要品味、体验京味文化，最好的方式是走进胡同，近距离接触北京居民的生活。如果有时间，那就背上照相机，迈开双腿，走进胡同、走进街巷，去亲身体验京味文化的魅力吧。

　　Many tourists to Beijing prefer to stroll in hutongs, taste Beijing roast duck, listen to Beijing opera, or even go to park to join the singing of local people. In this way, they feel they are experiencing local culture.

　　What is a Beijing culture? Beijing culture is local literature, art, architecture, language, folklore and people's view towards the world established on the bases of cultural phenomena of the inner city of Beijing. It features containing, kind, mild, humorous and philosophical. The best way to experience the culture is walking into hutongs and contacting with the common people there.

前门大街正对着昔日的皇城，当年是京城繁华的商业街市。前门大街有多家老字号商店，至今仍是百姓喜爱的购物场所。

Qianmen Street which leads directly to the former imperial palace and dotted with some old stores is still a popular shopping center in the city today.

胡同游
Hutong Tour

　　胡同源于蒙古语，自元大都开始，北京城有了胡同。在七八百年间，胡同构成了北京城的基本骨架，胡同里的一个个由院墙围合而成的四合院就是北京人的传统住宅。

　　The word hutong was from Mongolian. Hutongs came into being in the Yuan Dynasty. The framework of hutongs was formed in recent seven hundred to eight hundred years. The courtyards enclosed on four sides by hutongs are called Siheyuan, traditional living quarters for local residents.

位于北京市中心的什刹海地区，是老北京四合院保留区，由前海、后海、西海三个湖泊组成，夏天碧波粼粼，柳翠荷香，冬天冰平如镜，是天然的滑冰场。沿岸分布着保存完好的清朝皇亲贵戚居住的王府以及普通老百姓的民居，雕梁画栋与灰墙黛瓦和谐相处，高贵典雅中蕴涵着质朴平和，是老北京人的生活方式和京味文化特色最明显、最浓郁的地方。坐上胡同游的三轮车，在曲折蜿蜒的胡同里漫游，到四合院里尝尝老北京的饺子，是最受旅游者欢迎的"北京胡同游"。

Old Siheyuan has been well preserved in Shishahai area in downtown Beijing, where you may see prince's mansions and houses of common people along the lakes, and where you may feel a strong local cultural atmosphere. You may join a hutong tour traveling in narrow and long hutongs by pedicabs and walk into a shiheyuan to taste dumplings.

京剧

Beijing Opera

北京是被外国人称为"北京歌剧"的国粹——京剧的故乡。京剧有200余年的历史，起源于几种古老的地方戏剧，18世纪末开始在北京发展起来。京剧集歌、舞、念、打、音、美、文于一体，逐渐成为上至皇室、下至百姓，雅俗共赏的"国剧"。如今，北京既有位于长安街的长安大戏院这样的豪华戏院，也有前门梨园剧场和湖广会馆古戏园子这样的普通剧院。那里经常上演精彩的传统剧目和新编剧目。在北京的各大公园里，更随时可以找到一群群操琴打板、自得其乐地唱着京剧的北京人。

Beijing is the hometown of Beijing Opera. Beijing Opera has a history of more than 200 years. It originated from several ancient local operas and was later developed into Beijing Opera at the end of 18th century. Beijing Opera blending songs, dances, reciting, kongfu, music and fine arts together, was once popular among common people and imperial families as well. Today, traditional and newly revised operas are presented at luxurious Chang'an Theatre and ordinary Liyuan Theatre and Huguang Guildhall. You can easily find Beijing Opera fans in large parks in Beijing who are singing for their own enjoyment.

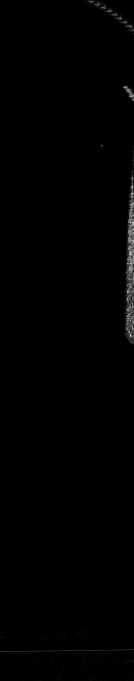

北京的魅力在于文化生活的丰富多彩,北京不仅是外来艺术充分展示的舞台,民族传统艺术也得到了很好的传承。中国的杂技世界闻名,在北京能欣赏到世界一流的杂技表演,《椅子顶》、《转碟》、《走钢丝》、《抖空竹》等杂技节目是地地道道的、精湛的民间传统艺术。

The charm of Beijing is from its rich culture life. External arts are presented and traditional art forms are well-preserved. Chinese acrobatics are well-known in the world. In Beijing, you may appreciate first class acrobatic performances like Chair Tip, Rotating Dishes, Steel Wire Walking and Hollow Bamboo Playing.

无论是外地游客还是外国游客，到了北京有一道美味不能不尝，这就是烤鸭。北京最著名的烤鸭店叫"全聚德"，这家老字号创建于130年前，其用挂炉方式烤制的烤鸭皮脆肉嫩，外表色泽鲜艳。现在，"全聚德"的连锁店已开到了外省和外国；另一家老字号烤鸭店叫"便宜坊"，以焖炉烤鸭为招牌。两家烤鸭各有特色，都是美味，所以，小小烤鸭居然成为北京风味餐饮的代表。

Tasting roast duck has already become a must for tourists. The most popular roast duck restaurant is called Quanjude, which has operated for 130 years. Now it has many chain restaurants at home and even in foreign countries. Another old roast duck restaurant is Pianyifang. Roast ducks served at these two restaurants are slight different in terms of flavor, but all taste good.

琉璃厂古文化街

Ancient Cultural Street at Liulichang

　　体验京味文化不要忘了去逛逛古文化街琉璃厂,那里也是最有北京特色的地方。琉璃厂位于和平门外大街,形成于大约200年前。琉璃厂曾经是中国传统字画、文房四宝、古旧书籍展示和交易的一个特定场所。现在,这条仿古的文化街是喜爱中国传统文化的中外游客和文化人"淘金"的好地方。

Don't forget to visit the cultural street at Liulichang when you are on a tour to explore local culture. Liulichang was once a special trade center for traditional Chinese paintings and calligraphy works, four treasures in study and old books. It was formed 200 years ago. Located on Hepingmenwai Dajie Street, it is an imitation of ancient cultural street, and a "gold mine" for both tourists and those who love traditional Chinese culture.

北京是多民族聚居区，不同民族的节庆也就成了北京的节日。当然，北京最重要的节日是春节。春节是中国农历新年，也是中华民族的传统节日。除夕之夜，传统是要全家团圆，包饺子、吃团圆饭。春节期间，各种类型的庙会上有许多民间艺术表演和让人垂涎的各种小吃，闻风而动的风车、一米多长的大糖葫芦是只有春节才能见到的北京民俗产品。

Beijing is a multi-nationality populated area. Nationality festivals are also Beijingers' festivals. Spring Festival is traditional Chinese festival. On the eve of Chinese New Year, the whole family is supposed to gather to make dumplings and have dinners together. During the Spring Festival, there will be many temple fairs, where you may watch folk art performances and taste various snacks. Colorful bamboo windmills and sugarcoated haws on one-meter long stick are exclusively for the festival.

现代都市
Modern Metropolis

北京作为历史文化名城而闻名中外，她像一座巨大的博物馆典藏着中华民族的悠久历史和灿烂文化。但是，北京又是一座非常现代化的都市，她的前进步伐紧扣着全球社会与经济发展的节奏。五十余年来，北京已经从一个纯粹的消费城市演变为一个在文化和科技建设方面领全中国风气之先，社会发展和经济总量在全中国名列前茅的现代化大都市，成为全中国人民向往的地方和闻名遐迩的旅游胜地。2008年即将在北京举行的第29届奥运会为这个古老而充满活力的城市勾画出更加美好的前景。

如果您与北京素未谋面，欢迎您来探访这座迷一般的城市；如果您来过北京，请您再来看看这座日新月异的东方名城。

Beijing is well known as a historical and cultural city. It resembles a huge museum that collects the long history and brilliant culture of the nation. Beijing is also a very modern city keeping abreast of the pace of world's social and economic developments. In 50 years, Beijing has transformed from a pure consuming city to a leading modern metropolis in China. It has become world tourist destination. The 2008 Olympic Games will provide more opportunities for this ancient and vigorous city.

四通八达的立交桥构成了现代北京的交通网络。
Cloverleaves link modern Beijing and have formed a transportation network in the city.

中央电视塔总高405米，塔旁一条碧水流过，风景如画。
405-meter-high CCTV Tower rises high into sky, and under the tower there is a picturesque small river flowing by.

北京国贸中心曾是北京的外资和合资公司最多、商务最繁忙的地方，但几年以后，以国贸中心为基点的北京CBD商务中心区将拔地而起，成为新的商务中心。
The Traders' Center, gathering many foreign and joint-venture companies, is now the busiest place in Beijing. The Central Business District, which will be set up in a few years, will become new business center in Beijing.

与"金街"王府井比肩而立的东方广场
Wangfujing, the "Golden Street" is standing side by side with the Oriental Plaza.

北京西客站是亚洲最大的铁路客、货运站，被誉为北京的"西大门"。
Beijing West Railway Station, known as the West Gate of Beijing, is the largest passenger and freight railway station in Asia.

西单文化广场是近年来新建的城市广场，位于繁华的西单商业区，以科技与文化为特色。

Located in downtown Xidan commercial district, Xidan Cultural Plaza is a newly built city plaza featuring technology and culture.

"金街"王府井是北京最著名的商业街，到北京的人没有不去王府井大街逛逛的。2000 年改造成步行街后，突出了王府井的历史和文化内涵。如今，"金街"白天人群熙攘，夜晚灯火辉煌，一片热闹景象。

Wangfujing, the "Golden Street", is the most well-known commercial street in Beijing. After renovation in 2000, the street emphasizes more of its historical and cultural contents. Now the "Golden Street" is crowded with people during the day and luminous and bustling at night.

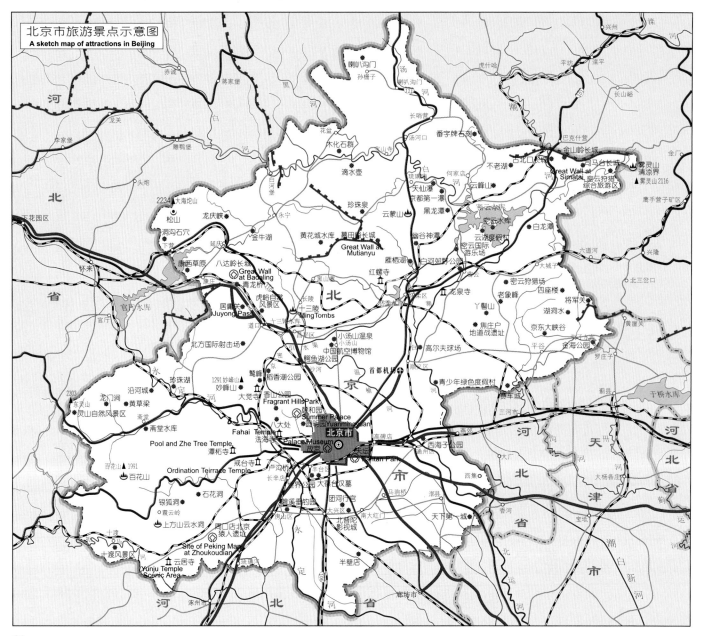

北京市旅游景点示意图
A sketch map of attractions in Beijing

河

北

省

北

京

市

河

北

省

河

北

省

天

津

市

河

北

省

金山岭长城

Great Wall at Simatai 密云狩猎
综合旅游区

雾灵山
清凉界
▲雾灵山 2116

密云国际
游乐场

密云狩猎场

京东大峡谷
金海公园

Great Wall at
Mutianyu

Great Wall
at Badaling

Juyong Pass

Ming Tombs

Fragrant Hills Park

Summer Palace
Yuanmingyuan

Palace Museum
北京市
故宫

Tiantan Park

Fahai Temple

Pool and Zhe Tree Temple

Ordination Teirrace Temple

Site of Peking Man
at Zhoukoudian

Yunju Temple
Scenic Area

96